First Ladies

Laura Bush

Joanne Mattern

ABDO
Publishing Company

visit us at
www.abdopublishing.com

Published by ABDO Publishing Company, 8000 West 78th Street, Edina, Minnesota 55439.
Copyright © 2008 by Abdo Consulting Group, Inc. International copyrights reserved in all
countries. No part of this book may be reproduced in any form without written permission from
the publisher. The Checkerboard Library™ is a trademark and logo of ABDO Publishing
Company.

Printed in the United States.

Cover Photo: AP Images
Interior Photos: Alamy p. 10; AP Images p. 31; Corbis pp. 4, 5, 11, 16, 21, 25, 27; Courtesy
    George Bush Presidential Library pp. 12, 13, 14, 15; Getty Images pp. 7, 9, 17, 18, 19, 20,
    23, 24; Courtesy White House Archives p. 6

Series Coordinator: BreAnn Rumsch
Editors: Rochelle Baltzer, BreAnn Rumsch
Art Direction & Cover Design: Neil Klinepier

Library of Congress Cataloging-in-Publication Data

Mattern, Joanne, 1963-
  Laura Bush / Joanne Mattern.
    p. cm. -- (First ladies)
  Includes index.
  ISBN-13: 978-1-59928-791-1
  1. Bush, Laura Welch, 1946---Juvenile literature. 2. Presidents' spouses--United States--
Biography--Juvenile literature. 3. Bush, George W. (George Walker), 1946---Juvenile literature.
I. Title.
  E904.B87M38 2008
  973.931092--dc22
  [B]
                                                                    2007009732

Contents

Laura Bush

Laura Bush became First Lady in 2001. Her husband is George W. Bush, the forty-third president of the United States. Mr. and Mrs. Bush have seen America through some very difficult times.

Laura Bush has proven to be her husband's strongest support.

Less than a year after President Bush was elected, America faced the tragedy of September 11, 2001. After that, the United States also endured serious **economic** problems. And, the country went to war against Iraq. Through these challenges, the First Lady supported her husband.

Mrs. Bush worked to help Americans stay strong, too. She spoke to families, encouraging them to support one another. Mrs. Bush also started several important programs to improve **literacy**. It is no wonder that Americans love this calm, determined First Lady.

Laura Bush's mother-in-law, Barbara Bush, once said, "Laura's quiet, but she accomplishes a great deal with that quietness."

Midland Girl

Laura Lane Welch was born on November 4, 1946. She was the only child of Harold and Jenna Welch. Their family lived in the small town of Midland, in western Texas. There, Harold owned a construction company. Jenna worked in her husband's office.

Two-year-old Laura loved to play outdoors with Bully, the family dog.

Laura's childhood was busy and happy. She learned to dance, swim, and play the piano. Laura also went to church, where she sang in the choir. And, she joined Girl Scouts.

Most of all, Laura loved to read. Her mother believed that reading was very important. So, she read to Laura all the time. Because of this, books would always be important to Laura.

Laura shares her love for reading with children around the world.

In her free time, Laura played with her friends. Together, the girls rode their bicycles and had sleepovers. Laura's friends liked playing at her house after school. She felt very safe while she was growing up.

A Hard Lesson

In 1961, Laura began attending Robert E. Lee High School. There, she earned straight As. She also got involved in student council and worked on the yearbook staff. During her free time, Laura and her friends liked to go driving, listen to the radio, and drink soda. They also liked to attend the school's football games.

On November 6, 1963, Laura was driving her father's car. She and a friend were going to a party. But, she drove through a stop sign and hit another car. Luckily, Laura and her friend were not hurt. However, the boy in the other car was killed. He had been a good friend of Laura's and a star athlete at her high school.

Some people thought Laura would get in trouble for causing the accident. But, the police determined that the road Laura had been driving on was dangerous. Since the accident was not Laura's fault, no charges were filed against her.

Still, Laura was very upset. She stayed home from school for several weeks. She also became quiet and careful. Laura thought a lot about life and death. She realized how important it was for everyone to make the most of their lives.

Laura's accident made her realize how special life is. So, she used her
role as First Lady to help others improve their lives.

The Right Fit

Laura had always wanted to be a teacher. After graduating from high school in 1964, Laura began attending Southern Methodist University in Dallas, Texas. Laura enjoyed college. She had many friends, and her dormitory room was always a fun place to be.

A librarian's job can be fun, but it is also a lot of work. Laura's love for books helped her succeed at her job.

Laura worked hard and did well in her classes. In 1968, she graduated from Southern Methodist University with a degree in education. After a summer in Europe, Laura started her first job as a third-grade teacher in Dallas. She moved to Houston, Texas, to teach second grade one year later.

After a while, Laura realized she wanted to be a librarian. So in 1970, she began taking classes at the University of Texas in Austin.

She received her library science degree in 1973 and moved back to Houston. There, she began working at a public library.

However, Laura soon missed working with children. So in 1974, she moved back to Austin to work as an elementary school librarian. She helped children at the school learn the importance of reading. At last, Laura knew what kind of work she loved best!

Laura loved helping children enjoy books. This inspired her to begin many wonderful literacy programs.

Meeting George

During the summer of 1977, Laura went home to Midland to visit her parents. Some of her friends invited her to a barbecue. They wanted her to meet a man named George W. Bush. Her friends had tried to introduce George and Laura before. However, Laura did not think they would have anything in common.

This time, Laura agreed to meet George. The two liked each other right away! Laura realized that she and George had more in common than she had thought. Both of them loved to have fun and be around their friends. George also made Laura laugh.

George and Laura had a whirlwind romance. They dated for only three months before getting married.

George and Laura were both 31 years old at the time of their wedding.

George and Laura fell in love very quickly. On November 5, 1977, they married. After the wedding, Laura left her job in Austin. She moved back to Midland with her husband. Her life was about to change forever.

A Special Family

Mr. Bush came from a political family. His father, George H.W. Bush, had held many government jobs. Mr. Bush wanted to work in politics, too. Soon after the wedding, he ran for Congress. Mrs. Bush traveled with him during the campaign. However, he lost the election.

Meanwhile, Mr. and Mrs. Bush had things on their minds besides politics. In 1981, the couple found out they were going to be parents of twins!

Jenna and Barbara Bush were born on November 25, 1981. Their parents named the girls Jenna Welch and Barbara Pierce, after their own mothers. Mrs. Bush was very busy

Mr. Bush was proud of his wife and his new twin daughters.

Mr. and Mrs. Bush spent their honeymoon campaigning from the back of a truck!

taking care of the babies. Her husband was busy running his oil company and helping with the babies, too.

In 1981, Mr. Bush's father became vice president of the United States. In 1986, he decided to run for president. He asked his son and daughter-in-law to help with the campaign. The whole family worked hard. In November 1988, their hard work paid off. George H.W. Bush was elected president of the United States!

The Governor's Wife

Mr. Bush had loved working on his father's presidential campaign. He soon wanted to run for office again, too. In 1993, Mr. Bush announced he would run for governor of Texas.

Mrs. Bush knew her husband had many ideas about how to improve life for Texans. They worked together during the campaign. Mr. Bush often asked his wife how he was doing. She was not afraid to tell him if he needed to improve his work.

In 1994, Mr. Bush won the election! The following January, the family moved into the governor's mansion in Austin. Being the governor's wife was a big change for Mrs. Bush. She did not want to be

At first, Mrs. Bush felt shy in front of big groups. But, she soon began to enjoy making public appearances with her husband.

famous, and she did not like to speak in public. But as First Lady of Texas, she was now a public figure.

Mrs. Bush wanted to help the people of Texas lead better lives. As a former teacher and librarian, she knew the importance of **literacy**. So in 1995, Mrs. Bush started a program to help families learn to read.

The Gift of Books

Laura Bush believes that "every child in America should have access to a well-stocked school or community library." So, the Laura Bush Foundation for America's Libraries was created. This foundation works to bring books to inner-city, rural, school, and community libraries.

Sharing her love for libraries and books became Mrs. Bush's mission long before she was America's First Lady. As First Lady of Texas, Mrs. Bush founded the Texas Book Festival. This annual event features local and national authors. Funds raised at the festival are given to Texas libraries for expanding book collections and promoting literacy. Since 1996, the festival has raised almost $2 million to support its mission.

Mrs. Bush also started the National Book Festival to promote reading. She said, "A love of books, of holding a book, turning its pages, looking at its pictures, and living its fascinating stories goes hand-in-hand with a love of learning." Mrs. Bush hosted the first event in 2001. It featured more than 60 award-winning authors and a children's reading hour. Since then, the festival has grown into a national celebration of literacy.

Election Trouble

The Bushes were popular in Texas. But Governor Bush wanted to do more. In 1999, he announced he would run for president of the United States. Mrs. Bush worried that it might be hard on their family if her husband became president. She wondered if their daughters would have normal lives. Still, Mrs. Bush wanted to help her husband win.

On November 7, 2000, Americans placed their votes for the next president. Many people voted for Governor Bush.

The 2000 election drew a high number of voters in every state. Floridians struggled to cast their ballots.

But many others voted for his opponent, Vice President Al Gore. At first, no one knew who the winner would be.

The race was very close! Only a recount of the votes in Florida would determine the next president. However, many people had problems with the way Florida held the election. Some complained that the **ballots** were difficult to understand. Others said they could not vote at all.

Government officials in Florida began recounting their state's votes. But on December 12, the U.S. **Supreme Court** stopped the recount. The court finalized the election and declared Mr. Bush the winner. He was only the second son of a president to become president himself.

Mrs. Bush enjoyed the crowds at a parade in Washington, D.C., before her husband took the presidential oath.

National Tragedy

The president and First Lady settled into life at the White House. Mrs. Bush was happy to continue her **literacy** programs. As First Lady of the United States, she could now help children all over the nation learn to read!

However, not everything went so well. Just nine months after President Bush took office, a terrible tragedy struck America. On September 11, 2001, **terrorists** flew two airplanes into the World Trade Center in New York City, New York. Soon afterward, another airplane flew into the **Pentagon**. Yet another crashed into a field in Pennsylvania. Thousands of people were killed in these attacks. Suddenly, the nation was in a state of emergency.

After September 11, Mrs. Bush focused on reassuring Americans they were safe. Soon, she was called "comforter in chief."

Government officials did not know if there would be more attacks. They worried about the president's safety. So, the officials wanted the president and First Lady to go to a safe, secret place. But the Bushes refused. Instead, they stayed at the White House.

President and Mrs. Bush guided the United States through the tragedy. When the president learned the **terrorists** were from a group based in Afghanistan, he led an attack against that country. The First Lady supported her husband's decision. She wanted Americans to feel safe again. So, she visited schools and asked parents to comfort their children.

President and Mrs. Bush visited the September 11 disaster sites and spoke to survivors and rescue workers. They mourned for the victims, their families, and the country.

Family Ties

Even while Mrs. Bush helped America face the terrible days after September 11, her family always came first. Her daughters, Jenna and Barbara, were not used to being in the public eye. The twins wanted to have normal lives while they were in college. Their parents did their best to protect the girls from the **media**.

The First Lady also faced painful days with her own parents. Her mother suffered from **cancer** but recovered. Then, her father became sick with **Alzheimer's disease**. Mrs. Bush helped her mother take care of him whenever she could. After her father died, the First Lady helped her mother move into a new home. No matter what, family was most important.

The president valued family, too. He believed in his wife's ideas. He also enjoyed hearing Jenna and Barbara's opinions. President Bush felt that the strong women in his family helped him succeed.

Mrs. Bush loves spending time with her daughters, whether they are
on their Texas ranch or traveling to foreign countries.

A Second Term

As President Bush's first term was coming to an end, he decided to run for reelection. But under his leadership, the United States had begun fighting a war with Iraq in 2003. Many Americans opposed this war. They did not like the way the president and other government officials handled the fighting.

President Bush faced a tough campaign to win reelection. His main opponent was U.S. Senator John Kerry. Senator

John Kerry did not agree with all of the president's ideas. Still, the First Lady treated him with respect during the campaign.

Kerry's ideas were very different from the president's. The two competed in a tense campaign, and the nation became divided.

Many people worried that the 2004 election would not have a clear winner. President and Mrs. Bush worked hard to make sure

that did not happen. They traveled all over the nation and met many different Americans. The president stood by his beliefs. He wanted people to know that he would not change his mind about important issues.

The election was close. However, it was not as close as the race in 2000. The day after the election, George W. Bush was declared the winner!

Laura's Future

After the 2004 election, the First Lady was happy to return to the White House. She continued to promote **literacy** for all Americans. She also remained supportive of her husband. The couple traveled throughout the country and the world to meet with other leaders.

Mrs. Bush also made time for her family. Her daughters graduated from college in 2004. After working on their father's campaign, the young women both started new jobs. Their mother felt proud, but sad, to see them leave home.

Mrs. Bush's friends also remain important to her. She still has close friends from her childhood in Midland. Every summer, the women go on a camping trip. Mrs. Bush enjoys these times. She can just be Laura Bush, instead of the First Lady of the United States.

It is clear that President and Mrs. Bush are a strong team. Together, they faced one of America's biggest tragedies. They led the nation through dark days. The Bushes also raised a strong family and kept ties with their childhood friends. Laura Bush is proud to be an American. And, she is proud to be a First Lady.

The Bushes enjoy an afternoon hike on their Texas ranch with Spot, their springer spaniel.

Timeline

1946	Laura Lane Welch was born on November 4.
1961–1964	Laura attended Robert E. Lee High School.
1964–1968	Laura attended Southern Methodist University.
1968	Laura began her first teaching job.
1970–1973	Laura attended the University of Texas.
1974	Laura began working as a school librarian.
1977	Laura married George W. Bush on November 5.
1981	The Bushes' twin daughters, Jenna and Barbara, were born on November 25.
1995–2000	Mr. Bush served as governor of Texas.
1995	Mrs. Bush began her work for literacy programs.
2001–2009	Mrs. Bush acted as First Lady, while her husband served as president.
2001	Terrorists attacked the World Trade Center on September 11; President Bush led an attack against Afghanistan.
2003	The United States went to war against Iraq.

Did You Know?

Two of Laura's favorite childhood books were *Caddie Woodlawn* and *Little House on the Prairie*.

Mrs. Bush grew up in the same town as her husband. They even lived in the same apartment complex after college, without ever meeting!

Mrs. Bush's favorite color is blue.

Mrs. Bush is the second First Lady to hold an advanced college degree.

Mrs. Bush is the only First Lady to be the mother of twins.

The Bushes have had a wide range of pets. They include two Scottish terriers, Barney and Miss Beazley; a cat named India; and even a Texas longhorn named Ofelia!

Mrs. Bush's favorite pastimes are reading and gardening.

Mrs. Bush loves to go hiking and camping.

In November 2001, Mrs. Bush became the first First Lady to give the weekly presidential radio address. She used the opportunity to discuss the need for equal rights for men and women in Afghanistan.

President and Mrs. Bush call each other "Bushie."

Glossary

Alzheimer's disease - an illness that causes forgetfulness, confusion, and overall mental disintegration.

ballot - a piece of paper used to cast a vote.

cancer - any of a group of often deadly diseases characterized by an abnormal growth of cells that destroys healthy tissues and organs.

economy - the way a nation uses its money, goods, and natural resources.

literacy - the state of being able to read and write.

media - a form or system of communication, information, or entertainment that includes television, radio, and newspapers.

Pentagon - a five-sided office building in Arlington, Virginia. It is home to the headquarters of the U.S. Department of Defense.

Supreme Court - the highest, most powerful court in the United States.

terrorist - a person who uses violence to threaten people or governments.

Web Sites

To learn more about Laura Bush, visit ABDO Publishing Company on the World Wide Web at **www.abdopublishing.com**. Web sites about Laura Bush are featured on our Book Links page. These links are routinely monitored and updated to provide the most current information available.

Index

MONDAY